The Numpy Pocketbook: Essentials on the Go

Table of Contents

Chapter 1: Getting Started with Numpy

What's Numpy?

Numpy, standing for Numerical Python, is the cornerstone library for numerical computations in Python. Providing powerful array objects, it's the backbone for many scientific computing tasks.

Why Numpy?

- **Performance:** Native Python lists can be slow. Numpy arrays are stored more efficiently and allow for faster operations.

- **Flexibility:** Perform operations on entire arrays without the need for loops.
- **Ecosystem:** Many data science and machine learning libraries, like Pandas and Scikit-learn, are built on top of or integrate well with Numpy.

Installing Numpy:

It's a breeze to get started. If you're using `pip`, just run:

```
pip install numpy
```

Or, for Conda users:

```
conda install numpy
```

Your First Numpy Array:

Once installed, you can create your first array:

```
import numpy as np
my_array = np.array([1, 2, 3, 4, 5])
print(my_array)
```

Output: `[1 2 3 4 5]`

Key Takeaways:

- Numpy is essential for numerical tasks in Python, providing a more efficient way to handle data than native Python structures.

- It seamlessly integrates with other major data science tools.

- Getting started is as simple as installing the library and creating your first array.

Chapter 2: Mastering Arrays

The Numpy Array:

At the heart of Numpy is the ndarray (n-dimensional array), a homogenous and grid-like data structure. Unlike Python lists, all elements in an ndarray are of the same type, ensuring efficient storage and fast operations.

Creating Arrays:

You can create arrays in several ways:

From Python lists:

```python
import numpy as np
arr_from_list = np.array([1, 2, 3, 4])
```

Using built-in functions:

- Zeros: **np.zeros(3) -> [0. 0. 0.]**

- Ones: **np.ones(3) -> [1. 1. 1.]**

- Range: **np.arange(4) -> [0 1 2 3]**

Array Attributes:

Every array has attributes like ***shape, size***, and

dtype:

```python
arr = np.array([[1, 2], [3, 4]])
print(arr.shape)   # (2, 2)
print(arr.size)    # 4
print(arr.dtype)   # int64 (or equivalent)
```

Accessing Elements:

Array elements can be accessed by indexing:

```python
arr = np.array([1, 2, 3, 4])
print(arr[0])    # 1
print(arr[-1])   # 4
```

For multi-dimensional arrays, use comma-separated indices:

```python
matrix = np.array([[1, 2], [3, 4]])
print(matrix[1, 0])  # 3
```

Basic Operations:

Arrays allow element-wise operations:

```
a = np.array([1, 2, 3])
b = np.array([4, 5, 6])
print(a + b)  # [5 7 9]
print(a * 2)  # [2 4 6]
```

Key Takeaways:

- Numpy arrays, **_ndarray_**, are the core components of the library, allowing efficient data storage and operations.
- You can create, inspect, access, and perform basic operations on arrays with ease.

Chapter 3: Shape & Transform

Understanding Shape:

An array's shape tells us its dimensions. For a 2x3 matrix (2 rows and 3 columns), the shape would be **(2, 3)**. You can inspect this with the *shape* attribute:

```python
arr = np.array([[1, 2, 3], [4, 5, 6]])
print(arr.shape)  # (2, 3)
```

Reshaping Arrays:

Change the dimensions of an array without altering its data:

```python
arr = np.array([1, 2, 3, 4, 5, 6])
reshaped = arr.reshape(2, 3)
print(reshaped)
# Output:
# [[1 2 3]
#  [4 5 6]]
```

Flattening Arrays:

Transform a multi-dimensional array into a 1D array:

```
arr = np.array([[1, 2, 3], [4, 5, 6]])
flattened = arr.flatten()
print(flattened)  # [1 2 3 4 5 6]
```

Broadcasting:

Numpy's way of handling operations on arrays of different shapes. It automatically expands the smaller array for the operation:

```
a = np.array([[1, 2], [3, 4]])
b = np.array([1, 2])
print(a + b)
# Output:
# [[2 4]
#  [4 6]]
```

Transposing:

Switch rows with columns:

```
arr = np.array([[1, 2, 3], [4, 5, 6]])
transposed = arr.T
print(transposed)
# Output:
# [[1 4]
#  [2 5]
#  [3 6]]
```

Stacking and Splitting:

Combine multiple arrays or split one into parts:

```python
# Vertical Stack
a = np.array([1, 2, 3])
b = np.array([4, 5, 6])
stacked = np.vstack((a, b))
print(stacked)
# Output:
# [[1 2 3]
#  [4 5 6]]

# Horizontal Split
arr = np.array([[1, 2, 3, 4], [5, 6, 7, 8]])
split = np.hsplit(arr, 2)
print(split[0])
# Output:
# [[1 2]
#  [5 6]]
```

Key Takeaways:

- The shape of an array defines its dimensions and can be easily modified.
- Broadcasting simplifies operations on arrays of different sizes.

- You can reshape, flatten, transpose, stack, and split arrays to fit your needs.

Chapter 4: Insights from Data

Descriptive Statistics:

Before diving deep into data analysis, it's essential to understand the basics about your dataset. Numpy offers various functions to help with this.

Mean & Median: Central tendency measures.

```
arr = np.array([1, 2, 3, 4, 5])
print(np.mean(arr))  # 3.0
print(np.median(arr))  # 3.0
```

Standard Deviation & Variance: Measure of data spread.

```
print(np.std(arr))  # 1.414
print(np.var(arr))  # 2.0
```

Min & Max Values: Finding the smallest and largest values.

```
print(np.min(arr))  # 1
print(np.max(arr))  # 5
```

Data Summarization:

Summarize data using aggregation functions.

```
# Sum and Product
print(np.sum(arr))  # 15
print(np.prod(arr))  # 120
```

Unique Values & Counts:

To understand the distinct elements and their frequencies:

```python
data = np.array([1, 2, 3, 2, 1, 4])
unique, counts = np.unique(data, return_counts=True)
print(unique)  # [1 2 3 4]
print(counts)  # [2 2 1 1]
```

Correlation:

Measure the linear relationship between datasets.

```python
x = np.array([1, 2, 3, 4, 5])
y = np.array([2, 3, 4, 5, 6])
corr = np.corrcoef(x, y)
print(corr[0, 1])  # 1.0, indicating a perfect linear relationship.
```

Sorting Data:

Organizing datasets in a specific order.

```
arr = np.array([3, 1, 4, 2])
sorted_arr = np.sort(arr)
print(sorted_arr)  # [1 2 3 4]
```

Key Takeaways:

- Numpy provides powerful functions to extract insights from data.
- Basic statistics can help understand the nature and distribution of your dataset.
- Functions like *unique*, *corrcoef*, and *sort* aid in advanced data analysis.

Chapter 5: Matrix Wonders

Matrix Basics:

In Numpy, matrices are essentially 2D arrays. They are fundamental in various fields like physics, engineering, and computer graphics.

Matrix Creation:

Make a 2D array (matrix) just like you'd make a 1D array:

```python
mat = np.array([[1, 2], [3, 4]])
print(mat)
# Output:
# [[1 2]
#  [3 4]]
```

Matrix Multiplication:

The dot product of two matrices:

```python
A = np.array([[1, 2], [3, 4]])
B = np.array([[2, 0], [0, 2]])
result = np.dot(A, B)
print(result)
# Output:
# [[2 4]
#  [6 8]]
```

Element-wise Operations:

Perform operations on corresponding elements of matrices:

```
print(A * B)
# Output:
# [[2 0]
#  [0 8]]
```

Matrix Transposition:

Swap rows with columns:

```
print(A.T)
# Output:
# [[1 3]
#  [2 4]]
```

Determinant and Inverse:

Fundamental in linear algebra:

```
det = np.linalg.det(A)
inverse = np.linalg.inv(A)
print(det)      # -2.0
print(inverse)
# Output:
# [[-2.    1. ]
#  [ 1.5 -0.5]]
```

Eigenvalues and Eigenvectors:

They have essential properties and applications, especially in physics and engineering:

```
eigenvalues, eigenvectors = np.linalg.eig(A)
print(eigenvalues)
print(eigenvectors)
```

Matrix Decompositions:

For instance, the LU decomposition:

```
P, L, U = np.linalg.lu(A)
print("L:\n", L)
print("U:\n", U)
```

Key Takeaways:

- Matrices are central in Numpy and have a wide range of applications.

- Whether it's multiplication, finding the determinant, or decompositions, Numpy makes matrix operations intuitive and straightforward.

Chapter 6: Tips, Tricks & Pitfalls

Tips, Tricks & Pitfalls

View vs. Copy:

When slicing arrays, Numpy returns views rather than copies, which can lead to unintended modifications:

21

```
original = np.array([1, 2, 3, 4])
slice = original[1:3]
slice[0] = 99
print(original)   # [1 99 3 4]
```

To avoid this, use the **copy()** method.

Avoid Using Loops:

Numpy is optimized for vectorized operations. Instead of iterating over arrays, leverage Numpy's functions:

```
# Slow
result = []
for i in range(len(original)):
    result.append(original[i] * 2)

# Fast
result = original * 2
```

Broadcasting Pitfalls:

While broadcasting is powerful, it can lead to unexpected results if shapes aren't compatible:

```python
a = np.array([1, 2, 3])
b = np.array([1, 2])
result = a + b  # This will raise a ValueError
```

Always be cautious with shapes when leveraging broadcasting.

Memory Usage:

Large arrays can consume significant memory. Use data types efficiently:

```python
# This uses more memory
float_arr = np.array([1, 2, 3], dtype=float)

# This uses less memory
int_arr = np.array([1, 2, 3], dtype=int)
```

Set Operations:

Numpy provides intuitive set operations:

```python
a = np.array([1, 2, 3, 4])
b = np.array([3, 4, 5, 6])
print(np.intersect1d(a, b))   # [3 4]
print(np.union1d(a, b))       # [1 2 3 4 5 6]
```

Know the Documentation:
Numpy's documentation is rich and provides insights into functions, methods, and best practices. Bookmark it!

Key Takeaways:
- Be aware of the distinction between views and copies in Numpy.
- Always prefer vectorized operations over loops for efficiency.
- Understand broadcasting to avoid shape mismatches and errors.
- Optimize memory usage by selecting appropriate data types.

Chapter 7: Numpy in the Wild

Numpy in the Wild

Interfacing with Other Libraries:

Numpy arrays easily integrate with many popular libraries like Pandas, Matplotlib, and Scikit-learn:

```
import pandas as pd
dataframe = pd.DataFrame(np.array([[1, 2, 3], [4, 5, 6]])
```

Image Manipulation with Numpy:

Images can be represented as arrays (especially grayscale). Manipulating them becomes intuitive:

```
from PIL import Image
img = Image.open('sample.jpg')
img_array = np.asarray(img)
# Manipulate the image, like setting the red channel to
img_array[..., 0] = 0
new_img = Image.fromarray(img_array)
new_img.show()
```

Audio Data Handling:

Audio signals can be seen as 1D arrays. Libraries like *librosa* can turn audio into Numpy arrays for analysis.

Numpy with SciPy:

While Numpy provides a foundation, SciPy builds upon it, offering additional methods for optimization, integration, and more.

Performance Tuning with Numba:

For computationally heavy tasks, **Numba** can JIT compile Python code, further optimizing Numpy operations.

Neural Networks with Numpy:

Before deep learning frameworks became mainstream, prototyping neural networks often started with Numpy:

```python
def sigmoid(x):
    return 1 / (1 + np.exp(-x))

inputs = np.array([0.5, 0.6, 0.7])
weights = np.array([0.1, 0.2, 0.3])
output = sigmoid(np.dot(inputs, weights))
print(output)
```

Key Takeaways:

- Numpy isn't an isolated tool; it's a foundation upon which many other powerful tools and libraries are built.
- From images and audio to advanced scientific computing, Numpy's versatility shines in various applications.
- Always be on the lookout for ways to integrate Numpy into other areas of interest.

It can often simplify and optimize your workflows.

Epilogue: A Numpy Odyssey

As we close this pocketbook journey, let's reflect on the essence of Numpy and its significance.

In the world of scientific computing and data analysis, Numpy has solidified its reputation as a foundational tool. Its power doesn't merely lie in its vast array of functions or efficient computations. Instead, its real strength emerges from its capacity to integrate seamlessly with various domains and tools, thereby broadening our horizons.

We've traversed from the basics of array manipulation to the intricacies of matrix operations. We've gleaned insights from data and navigated through potential pitfalls. In the wild terrains of real-world applications, from images to neural networks, Numpy's presence is felt, reiterating its versatility.

But remember, this pocketbook is merely a primer. The world of Numpy is vast, and there's always more to explore, learn, and master. The knowledge herein should serve as a launchpad, propelling you toward deeper explorations and innovative applications.

To the budding data scientists, engineers, and hobbyists, may your journey with Numpy be filled with discoveries and delights. Here's to the many computations, solutions, and innovations that await!

Thank you for joining us on this adventure, and until next time, keep crunching those numbers!